GW00862582

Polly and Friends

A Celebration of Dogs and Dog Life

by

Gill Pavey

© 2007 Gill Pavey

All rights reserved. No part of this publication may be reproduced in any form or by any means – graphic, electronic, or mechanical, including photocopying, recording, taping or information storage and retrieval systems – without the prior written permission of the author.

ISBN: 978-1-905451-51-7

A CIP catalogue for this book is available from the National Library.

First published 2007 in cooperation with Choice Publishing, Ireland
Tel: ++353 (0)41 9841551   Email: info@choicepublishing.ie
www.choicepublishing.ie

Dedication

This book is dedicated to the memory of Polly, my first Dalmatian, who died five days after bouncing around like a puppy and winning the Veteran Stakes at the Munster Utility Championship show at Clonmel. She became ill a couple of days later, and died on 13th July 2006 after her condition suddenly deteriorated. Sadly, before this book was published, I lost a second dog through a terminal illness that had become too much. Polo was simply the best dog anyone could have, and he is now buried beside Polly.

The book is also for dogs everywhere who give so much pleasure to their owners, and for the owners who have taken on rescue dogs and given them a second chance. A percentage of royalties from this book will be donated to dog charities both sides of the Irish Sea, to help with their good work.

Acknowledgements

I am grateful to the former Editor, Joan Richardson, and the Committee of the North of England Dalmatian Club for allowing the publication of material included in this book which was first published in the Carriage Dog Chronicle, the club magazine.
Cover photograph of Polly and the photos of Polly and Polo elsewhere are by Amy Cauldwell and reproduced with her permission. Visit her website, www.popspride.co.uk to see more of her work and pictures of her beautiful Dalmatian, Fraser, "Gwencarodale Pops Pride".
Photograph of "Skittle" on the "Active Dogs" section is by John Young and reproduced with grateful thanks. See his website at www.dephoto.co.uk.
Photograph of the two Borzois is by Photocall, (tel. 0044 (0) 191 4135697) and is reproduced with their kind permission.
Photographs of the Kelpie taking part in agility and flyball, the blue merle collie and puppy are by John Clarke of Sunnyside Photography (www.sunnyside-photo.co.uk)
Photograph of the Border Collie puppy "River" is by Jack Midgley.
Other photographs have been donated by the talented members of the excellent "Dogsey" website (www.dogsey.com) to whom I am extremely grateful. Thanks to Jules Furbank, Jane Odell, (website www.kaskanak.zoomshare.com), Emma Heslop, Paige Lumpkin (website at www.cockers.biz), Alexandra Lang, Becky Smith, Heather Waite (website www.kirkhampetventre.co.uk), Rebecca and Darren

Crosby, Rachel Atkin, Eleanor MacDonald, Dani Dinwoodie, Emma Brackenridge, Michelle Thomis, Shelley Watson, Phil Jerrard-Dinn & Patch Guipago for sharing photographs of their stunning dogs.
Last but not least - the poem "Ears" was originally written by Ann MacDonald, aided and abetted by Dylan, Doogle and Duncan.

Photo of Mia by Jane Odell

This is a celebration of dog life, the ups and downs, the good the bad and the sad, so be prepared to laugh and cry but above all enjoy – you may recognise your own dog hidden in these pages. After all, the dogs wrote most of this book with a little interpretation from me. I hope I got it right.

Gill Pavey
Granard,
Co. Longford
Ireland
© 2007

Inca as "Lechien"
Photo Rebecca and Darren Crosby

Introduction

There are working dogs, those who guard, sniff out drugs and accelerants, chase suspects, hunt, put up, flush out and retrieve, pull sledges and carts, herd farm animals, act as mascots and film stars. There are sporting dogs who race, jump, dance, pose and demonstrate obedience. There are assistance dogs for the deaf, blind and wheelchair bound not to mention their part in pets as therapy. Finally, there are the pets, companions through and through, truly part of their family. Life for all will vary but one thing shines through – loyalty, hard work and a special bond.

It's not all serious though. Dogs will still be dogs at every opportunity and don't let us forget it. Clowns at heart, eager to please, how can you be sad when you are in the company of dogs? What can be better than a run across empty fields still wet from the dawn dew as the dogs gallop in ecstasy, following every scent with glee?

This book is split into sections – owners, dog life, puppies, grooming and vets, active dogs, crimes and punishment – and finally, the sad part – when we lose them. I still need a tissue when I read some of that section and I am sure that many of you will need one too. Much of the material is based on my own experience and thoughts, with heavy influence from my own dogs who give me unconditional love and inspiration. Working on rescue has given some inspiration on the darker side of dog ownership and the fight against cruelty and neglect continues.

I had a lot of fun writing this, and plenty of distractions when my own dogs felt that I had spent enough time at the computer and a walk was required. Impossible to ignore, they would march up and down catching my attention, bring my walking shoes, "talk" at increasing volume then butt me with their snouts until I gave in. Shrieks of joy would greet my "WALKIES" cry as I shut down the computer. Do they rule my life? Of course they do – and I wouldn't have it any other way.

So read on and enjoy – give your dog a hug, he deserves it.

Contents

Maia, with Isla (English Springer Spaniel) and Harvey (Bichon Frise), at Redcar beach
Photo: Miss E Heslop

Owners

The good and the bad

Mia with Diesel
Photo: Jules Furbank

None of us really know what our dogs think of us. Do they see us as easy pickings for food and walks at regular intervals, a chance to get the best place by the fire? This poem was inspired by a conversation after some young friends had been to see a film where animals "talked". Is this how our dogs see us?

Chatroom

I love to gossip and chat all day
It makes the world go round, they say.
Whether doggy or not, it's all the same
I can chat on any subject you name
As long as we all speak as every dog will
With growls and mumbles, oh! what a thrill
Understanding the way that we are
Communicating wide and far
Important matters for those with a tail
After all, we haven't quite mastered "e-mail"

I love to gossip and chat all day
To put the world to rights my way
But living with you is another matter
Each time I climb onto your lap for a natter
You tell me to go and lie in my bed
I've been there all night (was it something I said?)
I don't understand you, but for the odd word
Like SIT!!! And NO!!! as if I've not heard
I'm not deaf or stupid, nor wicked or lazy
It's just that I'm busy, and things become hazy.

I love to chat whenever I can
And if you, my owner, my greatest fan,
For just one short day in my life, or an hour
Could start to talk "dog", our friendship would flower
The first thing I'd tell you, once and for all,
That I really don't want to be chasing a ball
I'd rather be whispering speak nothings to you
Or listening to music, that's quite good too
But I've given up trying, it's as simple as that -
So now I've made friends with the family cat!

Photo: Jules Furbank

Owners are usually well meaning, if only they would consider life from the dog's point of view and not their own. The "fair weather walker" is a common sight on good days, for the true dog person look out of the window when it is raining and blowing a gale! From observing the ecstatic reactions from mine when a walk is announced, I believe that going out is probably the single most important aspect of a dog's life almost regardless of weather conditions. Not just for getting the tickle out of their toes, but also for the fascination of scent, the possibility of other animals to chase or meet. Some owners see this as a chore; I remember as a child making rash promises regarding a promised Beagle puppy, and my Mother pointing out that as she would end up walking it, her commitment had to be total, not mine. How wrong she was; we all walked "Toffee" and enjoyed many a good trek over the countryside, that's when Toffee didn't escape and we had to raise a search party which inevitably covered an even wider area! Needless to say, when we finally lost Toffee, my mother returned to her first love – gundogs.

The next poem, in quite a different style, was written to show the frustration of a dog who is only taken out in good weather, missing out on so many "dog" pleasures only to be found when it is wet. The beaches and fields are remarkably empty at these times, too!

Fair Weather Friend

Whenever I go for a walk with my owner
It always must be when the sun is out
Or at least dry and not too windy
And certainly full daylight.
"She" can then wear something fashionable
In case we meet some other folk on the way
Then she can be admired by all
While I am ignored in my natural finery.
On walks like this, the sun gets in my eyes
So I squint a lot, which makes it more difficult
To spot a rabbit, or rat or hare
Which panic and hurry towards the blinding sun
Where they breathe a collective sigh of relief
Seeing me rudderless, pointlessly staring
Trying to look as though I know what is what
But failing miserably, despite holding myself proudly.

Now if it has been raining, what a difference it makes
The whole of nature batters my senses
The scents are so strong I'm straight onto a "high"
Each blade of grass, refreshed by the dousing
Must be carefully inspected and I must take my time
To read all the messages left there just for me
Before leaving my mark for the next one who passes.
The earth is alive with smells telling a story
I can hardly contain myself, stopping and starting
Trying to choose just which one needs most attention
It's the most important part of the walk!
My owner does not appreciate the need for this
And my neck is sore from being tugged into action
She doesn't approve of frequent halts and delays
She just doesn't get it at all I'm afraid.
Her nose is shorter than mine, and perhaps just for show.....

I would love to be taken for a long walk in the rain,
Lashed hard by wind and soft driving drizzle
And it does rain a lot in the place where we live
So my fair weather friend denies me many walks
I just have to imagine what the damp earth may bring
And the enjoyment of communing so closely with nature
My coat is warm and largely waterproof
Which is more than can be said for hers, it's true!
So I wouldn't feel discomfort even in harsh weather
Not that I've ever had much chance to test it
And she won't let me out on my own at all
Unless it's a quick trot round the patch called the garden
There are some smells there, but with few visitors
They are scant, often stale and a poor compromise!
I see other dogs, out in all weathers, heads down sniffing
I am so jealous, I bark at them frequently.

On odd days we are caught in a shower, sometimes heavy
With any luck, we'll be well away from home at the time
Then she has to bear the dampness and misery for a while
(Which is how she views it), and she grumbles constantly.
I perk up, and suddenly the walk is much better
My tail starts to wag, there's a spring in my step
But she hurries along, anxious for home
Where I will be rubbed briskly with my own towel
And banished from the furniture for a while
Until I have dried off; my feet may be washed too.
One day I rolled gleefully in a cowpat while we were out
And was hosed down outside with cold water as I shivered
More from loss of dignity than unpleasantness
But in the end it was worth it for the pleasures enjoyed.
But .... why can't she see that I don't mind all weathers?
Why do some owners not understand "DOG?"

One of the great things about having a dog is that they are so non-judgmental about our appearance, they accept us for our hearts and generosity of spirit. They don't worry about fashion, never think we look ridiculous, tired, overweight or scruffy. They always still love us in the morning and remain faithful through the bad times as well as the good. There's a lesson in there somewhere, I think.

Imperfection

My mum thinks she's not perfect
She frets both day and night
About her lank hair
And the need for skin care
She thinks that she looks quite a fright.

Me, I'm nearly three now,
I'm several colours, not matched
With odd shaped big spots
And hundreds of dots
So I look as if I've been patched.

My mum went in the bathroom
And let out a scream of woe
She thinks she's fat
I don't know about that
But she says that it HAS TO GO!

Why does she think she's imperfect?
She has what nature dished out
It has worked well for me
As the whole world can see
I'm handsome, of that there's no doubt!

I wonder if she thinks I'm perfect
I love her with all of my heart
And perfection to me
Is what I can see
And to me, she just looks the part!

She so needs to give up this feeling
And threatening to go under the knife
We are both, in our way
Perfect specimens, I'd say
So let's get on and live this good life!

Not every owner has had a wealth of experience when they acquire a dog, for some it is the first time and despite many good books on the subject, they are never quite ready for what will happen. Perhaps the computer industry should have a go ......

THE "PC" DOG ?

If dogs were produced like computers, I wonder how they would turn out?

- Everyone would have to buy their puppy from the same source. Agents and dealers would be carefully set up around the world.
- Peripherals such as collars, leads and beds will be made by a different company and will never quite match the dog.
- Your puppy would probably be a lot cheaper if you bought it in the USA.
- However good your puppy was, within six months a newer better version would have been developed, rendering yours useless for any purpose.
- Whenever you gave the dog a command, it would look at you quizzically as if to say "are you sure?" (no change there then)
- From time to time the dog would lock you out and not let you back in until you had simultaneously produced a pound of tripe, patted it on the head and tweaked its tail. For some reason you would accept this as normal.
- Occasionally, executing a manoeuvre such as trotting a triangle or taking a jump will cause the dog to shut down and refuse to restart, in which case you will have to carry it out of the ring and re-enter in a later class.
- Each dog would be linked to a dustbin raid detector which flashes up a message "this dog has performed an illegal operation" every time a theft occurs. This could be activated up to three hundred times a day.
- Re-booting would take on a whole new meaning and would be banned.
- Every time the sun came out, you would look at the dog but be unable to see a thing.
- The dog would be subject to unexplained viruses and would need to be de-bugged periodically. This would be despite the hundreds of pounds spent over the years to avoid this happening.
- Whenever the dog broke down, you would pay a stranger £30 an hour for consultation which would result in nobody being any the wiser but a repeat appointment for the following week.
- Bytes would always be perfect so judges would no longer be required to see the teeth.
- You would have to press "start" to make the dog sleep.

Gracie-Lou Lumpkin
Photo: Paige Lumpkin

Fortunately, it will never happen! No amount of robotics would give us affection like our dogs do and what would have been the outcome when Polo kept me awake after a serious car crash, instinctively nudging me every time I drifted off and probably saving my life in the process. He was young at the time and up to that point had appeared to be a brainless clown, but that night he excelled himself and had an extra special place in my heart afterwards. There is a well-known story about a couple whose toddler went missing, the wife wanted to get rid of the dog which the husband had before they were married, and in the panic over the toddler nobody noticed that the dog was also missing. Eventually the little girl was found and sitting guarding her was the dog; he would let no-one near the child until her mother appeared. Needless to say, there were no further issues about the dog staying in the household!

There are some people who simply shouldn't be allowed to own a dog and it never ceases to humble me just how faithful a dog can remain under appalling conditions. The next poem illustrates the reality for many dogs with bad owners who neglect and abuse them. Luckily, for this dog, it was not as bad as it seemed but there are countless examples of cruelty and neglect uncovered each year and the fight against this treatment of dogs will continue.

Nightmare

I've woken, to kicking and cursing
My owner is finally home
I take it that such things are normal
Like my coat that has not seen a comb
It's filthy and stained and so smelly
And crawling with various bugs
I scratch myself often and deeply
My skin flakes on carpets and rugs.

He's drunk and is shouting pure nonsense
I take it that I am to blame
I'm thirsty and desperately hungry
I've not had a thing since he came
I'll just have to forage and track down
Any food, and drink from a puddle
Even if snacks are unsavoury
And leave my insides in a muddle.

He must have gone off to bed now
The house is so quiet and still
He'll be smoking and careless about it
While my efforts to sleep come to nil.
.......What is that smell and that crackling?
The house has a bright orange glow
There's flashing blue lights in the window
I cower and keep my head low.

Just as I think that it's over
The terror has reached its black peak
I wake up for real, and guess what?
I'm cosy, my coat *doesn't* reek
And I'm well fed, relaxed and well loved
My owner is stroking my head
Saying "you've had a bad dream, now it's over,
You're a good boy, now go back to bed."

It was just a bad nightmare, of course!
We are "man's greatest friend" so it's said
It couldn't be true that we'd suffer
To be starved, kicked and then left for dead
For the nightmare belongs to the shadows
The stuff of black fiction, so dire
I relax, and with a sigh of contentment
Settle down, in front of the fire.

Dedicated to those dogs for whom the nightmare is a reality

Diggory Lumpkin enjoys a rest
Photo Paige Lumpkin

Of course, there are canine bullies as well and it seems that the smaller the dog, the feistier the attitude. There was a widely reported incident in the UK newspapers some years ago, where a postman had been attacked by a dog, sustaining injuries which were bad enough to keep him from work for a while. The breed? A Yorkshire Terrier – thereafter called the Yorkshire terrorist, no doubt! So if you see a small innocent looking dog on the street – beware!

Boss

It's great to be the boss around here
I love to swagger and strut,
Nobody touches a thing that is mine
They're scared of this bold mutt!
When I appear along the street
Other dogs simply scatter
Just in case they've displeased me
Or failed on some other matter!

Even big shot Rotties and Dobes
Shake when I'm around
And any that care to challenge me
Regret it, I've always found.
At home it's just the same for me
I rule, there's no denying
I make sure that my owners know
Just how much I am trying!

But lately I've been wondering
If I give too great a sting
I command respect and fear it's true
But do I miss something?
If I was nicer to my owner
And let her rub my belly
Maybe I'd get a better deal
And get to see more telly!

Nah! I'd rather carry on
Being the king of the hill
Putting every other dog
Firmly through the mill
After all, it's good to know
When you're a small Jack Russell
It's not the size of dog that counts
It's threatening teeth and muscle!

Whatever the size or breed of dog, they head for your bed at the slightest opportunity and even the heaviest-footed beast can tiptoe into the bedroom without anyone noticing. Despite the sound advice of dog books that this is not a good idea on the grounds of discipline, many owners let the dogs on.

Three In A Bed

I love my two great lumps of dogs
Even if they snore like hogs
And when the time comes to retire
I have no choice but to admire
The way they spread out when they sleep
In no time flat there's not a peep
Happy and contented boys
Surrounded by their favourite toys.

A problem - despite a good report
They scorn the special beds I bought
At great expense from a good pet shop
Softest foam with fur on top
They much prefer to settle down
Spread out on my eiderdown
Which is an expensive, duck down quilt
They curl up on there, with zero guilt.

As they get there before I'm ready
One has in place his favourite teddy
Balanced firmly between front feet
Eyes tight shut, they look so sweet
They barely stir as I climb in
With knees bent high below my chin
I have about a foot of bed
I have no place to lay my head

I throw a toy and call out "fetch"
I have a second to try a stretch
Before they thunder up again
And shift me over, what a pain
The quilt is pegged, my back is bare
I'm left to chill in cooling air.
I'm using one dog as a pillow
My back's bent like an ageing willow

I'm going to get them off my bed
There's really no more to be said
I just can't take it any more
Dogs should sleep upon the floor
On a rug, that's how it should be
Not where they are, which is just for me
Should I change over to the chair?
I think there's far more room on there!

With grunts and shoves I give a heave
The dogs, though sluggish, up and leave
Until I'm settled, nice and straight
By then they're bored with such a wait
And fit themselves around my form
My goodness they are nice and warm
They squirm around and stretch at leisure
Back to sleep with sighs of pleasure.

I stay awake for quite a time
By then it's quite a pantomime
From lying with me head to toe
They've shifted round, like I don't know
So now they're slumped across my chest
Or whatever position suits them best
Before I realise and without warning
No time for sleep – it's already morning!

Three into two WILL go! Photo: Author

"Brynings Feadh Reah" – Felix
Photo John Clarke

Dog Life

Dogs being dogs

Breagh searches for anything tasty!
Photo: Phil Jerrard-Dinn

Dog life with humans varies according to the relationship, but the bond between man and dog leads to all dogs making a huge song and dance when you return, even if you have been away for a short time. Some show great anxiety when separated from "the boss" and the relief on their return is immeasurable. I know that mine are asleep by the time I reach the front door and probably remain so until they hear the car coming back up the lane. They certainly know my car from any other, so have a few minutes to compose themselves into pictures of abandonment and neglect before hurling themselves at me simultaneously with licks and nips of pleasure as the "pack" re-forms. I can hardly bear to leave them at kennels when I have to do so but their squeals of excitement when we arrive and discrete enquiries of the owner assure me that they actually prefer being there than with me at home! I am the one who feels abandoned ....

Welcome Home

I've been planning this moment for ever
You've been gone for such a long time
I've been sad and depressed
And been doing my best
To keep smiling, like everything's fine.

You're going to be here any minute
The others will just have to queue
I can't read a clock
Or a watch, now don't mock
But I know in my heart that you're due!

I'm ready for this great reunion
I'm prancing around in a state
When you walk through the door
I'll jump clean off the floor
Believe me, I simply can't wait!

I can see you! Why won't you come in?
It's me here, smiling and wagging
Preparing to jump
And scrabble, and bump
And give kisses galore without flagging.

At last! I'm baying with glee,
Welcome home, my very best friend
I'm excited and leaping
Behaviour in keeping
With spirits now well on the mend!

It's sad when you go out and leave me
I can't bear to be parted from you,
You're my sunshine, my flower
YOU WERE GONE A WHOLE HOUR!
(I think Blackie and Star missed you too!)

Reunited!
Photo: Shelley Watson

Of course, when their owners are not around, some dogs like to think they can do just as they please. I am convinced that they don't miss me at all while I am gone, but feel the need to make a huge fuss when I return, probably just to make me feel guilty.

Birthday Girl

I'm six! I'm sensible, clever and good!
I know what I can't do, and things that I should
I'm told I have offspring, some nearly three
It's strange that they're all related to me

I'm six, it's my birthday today, so there!
I'll celebrate by stealing a towel, if I dare
Followed by slippers, a scarf and a mop
Then lie by the fire in a big belly flop

So I'm having a party with biscuits all round
You're all invited but don't make a sound!
I've not told my owner, she won't understand
So its all a bit, well you know, underhand.

I've got to be sensible now I'm grown up
And set an example to visiting pups
So to show you how adult and quiet I've become
Here's one for the album, showing my tum!

"China"
Photo: Alexandra Lang

Wait 'Til I Get You Home

Those with the male of the species can fill a book with embarrassing tales, usually based on either toilet or reproduction functions, and many of the stories are unrepeatable! Everyone who owns a male has had the "get-your-attention" display of the private parts from a dog who is running out of patience while you chat to a friend, or the really emphatic "let-me-pee-on-your-leg-and-see-if-you-will-talk-to-me-then" tactic, which is certainly an attention grabber. Food is a well known hazard, but did you hear about the bitch who was offered a sticky teaspoon to lick and swallowed the lot? The owner telephoned the vet who just laughed and suggested that if nothing appeared from the rear after three days the bitch would have to be opened up. The vet presented the owner with the x-ray, the spoon and an even bigger bill.

Most dogs are totally uninhibited when it comes to bodily functions, no more so than the dog belonging to a regular exhibitor who was at the time showing him at Crufts for the first time. Half way round the triangle, the exhibitor sensed that the dog was not moving as fluidly as he had when they set off. In fact, in the second it took to realize this and glance at him, he had stopped altogether with the unmistakable arched back and a determined "I've got to do it NOW!" expression as a great pile emerged right on the hallowed green carpet. The exhibitor, who was not carrying a bag at the time, had to stop, beg a bag, clear the mess while the world looked on, then dispose of the obnoxious package. Eventually the pair were able to finish the remaining part of their round with an extra spring in the dog's step but a red-faced exhibitor who couldn't wait to leave the ring and the NEC.

At an Open show a few years ago, someone who had won two classes with a dog and a bitch was asking whether anyone would handle the dog for her for the Best of Breed. A man who was a bitch owner volunteered and was horrified when young Max cocked his leg expertly against the man's clean chinos, and before the fuss had died down Max repeated the process with pin point accuracy into a box of rosettes on the floor by the adjacent ring which was ready for another breed. The owner, meanwhile, was trying to melt into the background with her bitch pretending not to know the dog. Max continued grinning foolishly at her while being threatened with various physical impossibilities by the temporary handler and the steward from the next ring.

Visitors are a particular hazard to dog owners. It is only when you have people round for tea that your canine companion decides to rummage through the laundry basket for the piece of your underwear most in need of a wash and deposit it triumphantly at the feet of your distinguished guest, grubby side up. Human friends are often greeted warmly, and I use the term in it's literal sense, by the plunging of noses into crotches followed by a good snort of hot air.

You can also be embarrassed by other people's dogs. One kind hearted person offered to walk a friend's bitch with her own two, as the owner had 'flu. Walking down the side of a cornfield behind some houses, the dogs were running loose when the "guest bitch" suddenly decided to wriggle through a gap in the hedge and the dog walker dashed up to catch her, only to see the rear end disappearing into an open door of a nearby bungalow. The occupier, who had stopped briefly to speak to a neighbour, barely had time to raise her voice before the bitch re-emerged with half a pound of butter in her jaws, munching ecstatically. Claims that the bitch "was not mine, but belonged to a friend" were met by understandable disbelief by the witnesses to this daylight robbery. Via the village post office cum general store, the whole community knew what had happened within the hour and as the owner declared she was still "too weak" (from laughing probably) the dog walker had to purchase another pack of butter.

Another owner used to walk a couple at a local Country Park until the picnic season started when she became quite adept at whipping a couple of leads into a pocket and pretending to be a bird watcher, scowling at other dog owners as deprived picnickers were heard screaming for revenge. The triumphant pair trotting up to her with bulging jaws and wagging tails did give the game away though. Beaches were no better. Wisely avoiding the summer months, she would walk them during cold winter days, only to find that the dogs seemed to know that the hardy fishermen always had a substantial packed lunch. Well, at least it started that way .... In the end she had to walk on a friend's private land as reputations and compensation claims were getting out of hand.

The trouble is, you rant and rave and they just carry on wagging their tails and behaving like idiots until you can't be cross with them any more. Don't you just love 'em?

Sometimes what dogs do is just plain irritating but clearly not an attempt to deliberately wind their owners up. Ann MacDonald penned the following after noticing a trait in one of my bitches.....

Ears

Who says my ears don't sit right
I don't know where you've been
They're just the way I like them
Straight and thin and lean
I present them when I want to
It's just that I'm not sure
If I want to please you
Even though you implore
When I'm standing in the garden
Or when I'm feeling blue
I present my ears quite nicely
So I just say "ya boo!"
I'm going to have a think now
To ponder what to do
But please don't get your hopes up
I won't do it just for you
And I'm not being naughty
It's just that, don't you see,
I like the way my ears are,
It's just me being me!

Photo of Bella by Author

The great dog ritual is to go outside and relieve itself, except that nothing is quite so simple and mine have been on the point of bursting but refuse to do anything until the surrounding area is checked out thoroughly. Puppies find house training particularly strange and difficult, depending on how the owner has taught them and some accidents are inevitable until the message is clearly understood. Privacy seems to be important – just stand and watch!

Housetrained

We've just got to go into the garden
We've been waiting all night, you see
For a dash to the lawn
We've been ready since dawn
Planning where it's going to be.

But first we have to examine
And check if we've had a visit
Sniffing with care
To see who's been there
The sensations are quite exquisite!

Our owner comes into the garden
To see if we're ready to eat
But the girls are all shy
And always think "why
Can't we have paper, a chain and a seat?

Being a boy, things are different
We like to do it a lot,
Regardless of need -
And we pay little heed
To shrieks of "not in my pot!"

Mind you I am still such a baby
I'll go out and sniff more and more
But then dash back inside
As the door's open wide
And leave great golden pools on the floor!

"Nugget" (age 9 weeks)

Many dogs are required to travel in a car, whether it is the annual trip to the vet, a holiday or regular travel to events or access to better walks. Mine are well used to the crate in the car and leap in without fuss regardless of the length of journey. I worked out that they travel around 15,000 miles a year and often wondered what they thought about it.

Ramblings of a Travelling Dog

I've often thought, regarding cars
Why is it that "she" inevitably sits
In the front, where the view is better
But I must go in the back, with a friend.
I also like to see where we are going
Even if I don't know until we get there.
My friend went in the front once.
He said it wasn't up to much –
In fact, the seat was hard with ridges
So he had to curl up tight, to fit.
He also had to wear a harness
So he couldn't move around too much.
"She" sat still and ignored him, mostly,
Staring ahead and sometimes to each side
So he didn't get much benefit all in all
I felt much better when I noticed that.

It's not too bad in the back during daylight,
We can stare through the back window and see
Other cars which creep up too close behind
Occupants amused, seeing us cooped up in a cage
While we make indignant faces about it
We don't find this amusing at all
And need to campaign for a bigger car
Or at least our freedom to spread out a little
My friend takes up far too much room, in my opinion
I am sure I must be entitled to half the cage!
Sometimes I face forward, he backwards
That way we are sure to miss nothing
Although he doesn't always tell me what he's seen
So I keep to myself the fascinating fact
That "she" has opened some packet of food
And may pass some of it back where I am waiting.

Longer trips involve breaks on the way
Just as I am nicely settled and dozy
She stops, opens up and takes us both out
On some windswept hill with rain lashing down
Insisting that we relieve ourselves as she puts it
Getting impatient at our prolonged sniffing first
But certain procedures must be met, by a dog
So we take our time, amongst grumblings
And impatient jerks on the lead as we linger.
Then back in the cage to settle once more
Trying to remember who had which bit
Finding the bedding still warm from earlier
And yet it never seems to be the same
As it was before we had our few minutes out.
If my friend jumps in first, it is always the case
That he discourages me from entering, but I ignore him.

On the way back, with the forgotten water bowl
Slopping dampness into the bedding where I am lying
It is often dark as we bounce along country roads
Anxious for the journey's end and the return of normality
There is some kind of music and chat piped back to us
But we both try to sleep to make the journey go more quickly
Although in the darkness we have no concept of time
It seems never ending and we don't sleep that well
Interrupted by bright flashes as we pass through towns.
But always when we are nearing home, I recognise
The click-clack, click-clack noise that the car makes
Just before we turn into the narrow lane leading to HOME;
Hurray! I whine and squeal at the prospect
Of a good stretch before settling down for the night
Eating, though tired, then off to my bed.
Wondering where we might go tomorrow......

Some years ago I took my two dogs yachting on a vintage wooden ketch. It soon became apparent that one loved it, sitting on the coachroof with the wind lifting her ears, and the other simply hated it and cried to go home. It was a very short trip. I should have guessed that there would be problems when Max, on being asked to walk along the wooden jetty, suddenly glimpsed water below through the gaps in the planking and froze. The family had a Labrador many years ago and she was the same, which was a bit disappointing for a breed that generally likes water! Being in Ireland mine became accustomed to traveling on ferries when we visited the UK for shows, in fact I am sure that they were more relaxed about it than I was on the rougher trips. An exhibitor who visits Ireland from the Isle of Mann is able to fly with her dog sitting by her feet. Now that really is traveling in style .....

All I know is that when I acquired my first dog, I had an eight year old hatchback and within the space of only a few years had moved through an estate car, a camper van then a full blown motorhome with all luxuries. Polly, who was behind most of the vehicle upgrades, used to travel on the rear bunk so she could look out of the back whenever she fancied ....

It's a dog's life alright!

Pellow and Rye
Photo: "Photocall"

Isla, English Springer Spaniel, 4 Months Old
Photo: Miss E. Heslop

Puppies ....

Can't live without them, can't live with them!

Golden Retriever puppy
Photo: Becky Smith

Puppies are easily the biggest time wasters in the world. The first litter I bred was, obviously, the bitches first time as well and it was an unforgettable experience. This was inspired by Hannah, the bitch in question, who was the sweetest most loving bitch and also completely innocent of all things maternal until, much to her surprise, the litter arrived. She was an excellent mother and to this day probably has no idea where they came from.

Mother's Day

I've had the strangest experience
It was autumn, as I recall.
My friend Polo, a male,
Started sniffing my tail
That's really not like him at all.

And then it became even odder,
He started a brand new game
My mum she held tight
With all of her might
While I wriggled about, in vain.

For some time, nothing much happened
Except that I felt happy and calm
I went to the vet
For a scan, and yet –
I still didn't feel alarmed.

I gradually got fatter and fatter
Eating tons of my favourite food
I had gentle walks
And friendly talks
Which kept me in a good mood.

One January night, quite late
I panted and lay on my belly
Boy, did I feel ill
As I tried to lie still
My legs had turned into jelly.

My owner held on to my paw,
She smiled and looked into my eyes
Then a puppy appeared
Not as bad as I'd feared
So that's why I'd got such a size!

All through the night I laboured,
The litter was getting much bigger
By the time it was dawn
Nine pups had been born
And I was regaining my figure.

I was so proud to have all my puppies
Even though they caused me some pain
My mum says I'm clever
But I don't think I'll ever
Be speaking to Polo again!!!

Hannah and baby, six hours old.
Photo: Author

However you acquire a puppy, there is always the concern that an older dog already in the household will object to the new arrival through jealousy or the dislike of a "strange" dog in the house. Luckily, most dogs are enchanted with puppies and many find a new lease of life with having a new playmate. Puppies, of course, expect anyone and everyone to share their uncompromising view of life and play in particular, so launch themselves at anything living that they can get to – including cats who usually take it in very bad part!

Playmates

I've got a brand new playmate
Who I met the other day
His coat is black
He has the knack
Of showing me how to play

It's not that I've forgotten
How to bounce and bend,
But life's not great
Without a mate
And this boy's now my friend!

My mum thinks I am silly
She tells me so each week
But I'm just glad
Life's not so bad
I'm not one to be meek!

I'm told I will grow up soon
And playing will calm down
I think she's wrong
(now where's my Kong?)
I'll always be a clown!

But here's to my new playmate
You think he is the puppy?
He's FIVE YEARS OLD
And still so bold
I just think I'm so lucky!

"Turbo Charged" aka Trio
Photo: John Clarke

There's Something I Need To Tell You

Whether you share your home with other dogs, other pets or people, there comes a point where you need to tell them that a puppy is about to join the household. This needs careful handling to avoid a divorce, fluffed up cats or other existing residents threatening to leave home.

Photo: Jules Furbank

Owners of single dogs approach breeders worried that a new puppy might upset the existing adult, or the adult might flatten the puppy through carelessness. It seems that in most cases it is the resident adult that dives behind the settee every time the fearless and confident puppy comes into view rather than the other way around. An experienced, no-nonsense owner had two male dogs fairly close in age, no live-in partner or other dogs so the decision to introduce a third was relatively easy, so she thought. Unfortunately, the first two had been unusually easy to rear and the third was the puppy from hell, terrifying the older two into quick submission. For years, dog number three was convinced that his name was "Duncan-no". The owner said often that if Duncan had been her first dog, she would not have had another.

A breeder who already had five permanent residents had a litter in which there was one boy who caught her eye. The husband had manfully accepted the increasing numbers without too much complaint but the breeder was convinced that with the possibility of number six, he would crack under the strain especially when all were loose when he was trying to watch tv; after all, there's only so much room on a three piece suite. Nothing much was said until nearly all the other puppies had gone, then the breeder muttered about "running him on" until the summer which fell on unenlightened ears. The husband emerged from the lounge the next day with a grinning, triumphant puppy in his arms, and announced "this one likes me" ...... "funny you should say that", announced his wife who owned up at last.

Sometimes the arrival of a new puppy can make the existing dog very insecure and in need of reassurance that the newcomer is not going to take all of the owner's attention. It is so tempting to make a fuss of a new puppy and play with it at every opportunity leaving the older dog feeling somewhat left out. When Deccy arrived, I let him meet Polo gradually in an open space, and encouraged him to try out his new toys which were scattered around. Polo decided to trot off and bring back the oldest, scruffiest toy he could dig out from the bushes and dropped it at Deccy's feet as if to say, "the new ones are MINE this is yours!" Having asserted himself from day one, they were best of friends thereafter.

Am I Still Your Baby?

From the age of eight weeks I've been yours,
Six wonderful years of deep joy;
I'm your soul mate, I know
And I do love you so
But am I *still* your big baby boy?

Last year we had an addition,
A puppy so packed full of charm
I shared all my things,
Bones, balls and rings
Making sure he was safe from all harm.

As he grew bigger, he changed;
Grabbing all your attention, you see;
He'd throw me a glare
So I'd stay – well, right there –
While he got all the fussing, with glee!

I felt lonely and sad and depressed
Then one day you took me aside
And kissing my ear,
Said "you've nothing to fear"
And that's not a thing I will hide"

So now I sleep with you all night,
Stretched out alongside you, I'll stay,
While the other one's fate
Is to sleep in a crate
He's not got it ALL his own way!

He may be above me, the best
The "king of the hill"? ..well maybe..
But I know in my heart
He'll not play my part
I'm STILL your big soppy baby!

Photo of the late Polo: Amy Cauldwell

It is always fun bringing a new puppy out to training classes. Even the most experienced owner can expect routine humiliation from the mad thing spinning at the end of the lead, assuming the lead is not already forming a hitherto undiscovered cat's cradle. Whether obedience or ringcraft, the results are the same – highly entertaining for all the onlookers!

The Trainee

My puppy bitch who's black and white
On training nights, just takes flight
I've given up, it is too late
To teach her how to trot dead straight
She has a bound, a leap and jump
Landing with a mighty thump
She lurches here and there with joy
Just like some crazy wind-up toy
I'm becoming really miffed
With her moving crooked gift!

And as for standing, that's quite out
She'd rather somersault no doubt
And chew her lead with rolling eyes
She's just a devil in disguise
Show her teeth? She'll simply grin
And dare the brave to dive right in
Before she flops down on her back
And venture on another tack
Like wave her back legs in the air
By then I really couldn't care!

As long as she's happy, I am glad
She'll always be completely mad
I can't wait to take her to some shows
And I'm sure deep down, she really knows
It's a good day out with all her friends
Loving every hour she spends
Living life at near full speed
It's just a shame she takes no heed
She might do well if she slowed right down
But wouldn't it be boring...........

Whether you want to get the puppy back from the depths of a muddy field so you can go home, get him to stand to attention in the show ring, or simply display common courtesy to your friends when they admire him instead of gazing into the distance, there are various ways to grab his attention.

The most obvious is the use of a treat. Recalling a young dog from beyond yelling distance is a favourite pastime of many; a new owner, exasperated and voiceless through constant, fruitless calling decided that rewarding a recall with a treat was the way forward. The only trouble was, letting the dog know that it was available...... she was seen for a while very early in the mornings, jumping up and down, windmilling her arms wildly and bizarrely, shouting "bisssss.....cuit....!!!!" This seemed to work. For about a week.

At home, it is always embarrassing when you have a visitor who has come to admire this canine paragon that you have been banging on about in the pub for weeks. This entertaining, charming, playful love of your life sits by the window as though the end of the world is nigh, yawns noisily and refuses to come when requested. No amount of shaking toys, calling in a silly voice or rattling the biscuit tin will move him out of his bed, until the visitor is due to leave. Then the visitor gets an hour of attention crammed into two minutes with the owner's plaintive "he's not normally like this" following the fast retreating back. The owner slinks back inside to find the dog in full party mode and a picture of injured innocence, all in the same expression.

Squeaky toys – if you have any whole ones left, these provide endless fun and entertainment at home to puppies but for some reason they are embarrassed about it out in the big wide world. Knotted ropes have slightly more "street cred." Proffer a squeaky toy on the dog walking field and, like a small boy, he will pretend he is not with you and canter away to prove the point, but just try offering it to another dog and stand back. Well back.

Another dog is a real magnet, especially if it is about a mile away. Regardless of any evidence to the contrary, your puppy is currently deaf to all requests, pleas, threats to return until he has exchanged extravagant pleasantries with all other dogs in the vicinity.

You can always try hiding, so the pup will think he has lost you and come anxiously looking. One young lady out with her two youngsters who were running free, slipped on some ice and lay flat on her back, temporarily winded. Sure enough, the pups came lolloping over and sniffed her carefully. She opened her eyes to see them trotting off again, apparently satisfied that she wasn't dead yet and would probably get up eventually and take them home for their tea. When they were ready, of course.

"Now what did I do with that puppy?" Clayton ponders.
Photo by Eleanor MacDonald

Puppies, though totally delightful creatures and beautiful in every breed and type, can really test the patience of the new owner trying to turn the canine dynamo into a civilised pet.

Housemates

I'm sharing my house with a creature
Who has habits disgusting and strange;
She slurps when she's drinking
Drops crumbs without thinking
It's best to stay well out of range!

She screams without warning or reason
I wish I knew what was so wrong
I'm doing my best
But she's such a wee pest
Yet somehow we must get along!

Last night was the worst time of all
I couldn't sleep properly or well
She was up half the night
Wide awake and too bright
Dancing around, it was hell!

She clatters her way up the staircase
Then tumbles when coming back down
She thinks it's a game
She has NO real shame
It's embarrassing to live with a clown!

Do you think I should get some advice?
On how things should really be?
That could be just fine
If she was the canine
But I am the pup, SHE owns ME!

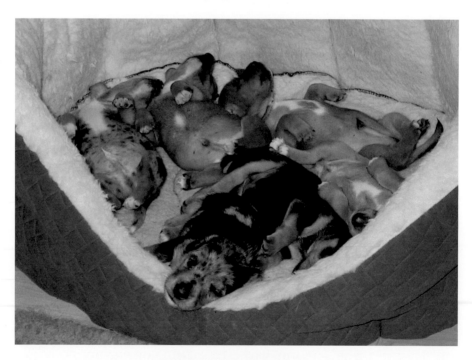

"Tired puppies"
Photo: Becky Smith

Breeding a litter for the first time is not for the faint hearted. I waited a number of years before doing this and as soon as the mating was done,

I went on many shopping trips for equipment and the other essential bits and pieces that the mother to be apparently could not live without. In the end, I think I was better equipped than the local vet! The due day arrived, and I sat with Hannah all day but although she was showing signs (according to the book – but how long can the bitch spend ripping up newspaper?) she was holding back. I settled in for a long night, reference book in hand, and watched her like a hawk. She fell asleep.

After a few hours she started to circle around inside the whelping box, and I noticed a bulge had appeared, but she seemed to be struggling to make the first delivery. Mindful of puppies getting stuck and other calamities, I rang the vet who came quickly even though it was the early hours of the morning by then. Of course, by the time she arrived the first puppy was safely delivered and Hannah, though a little surprised at this turn of events, was cleaning it up. As the vet had already come out, I put the kettle on and made some tea. As we chatted, the vet said – "look! I've just seen two tails!" Sure enough, the second puppy was born without us even noticing. Eventually she left, sleep being more important than a bigger fee, and I stayed up while the rest of the litter was born. The lights were dimmed, it was the middle of the night but it was a surreal experience and one that I will never forget. Hannah turned out to be very capable but glad that I was there, offering discrete assistance when necessary and towards the end, she became very tired so help was appreciated. By morning it was over, and Hannah was mother to thirteen puppies. We had lost one on the way, it had clearly lost the fight about a week before and when the vet returned mid morning to check the family out, she removed the tiny remains and Hannah didn't even notice. She was a very attentive mother and it was a struggle to get her outside when necessary for a comfort break, allowing me a few minutes to change the bedding before she tried to beat the door down and hollered to be let back in.

Hannah had eleven sons and two daughters, one of which I kept, and she appears in this book as Bella with the flyaway ears. All went to excellent homes after eight weeks of very hard work, especially after they were three weeks old and Hannah decided that I could take over. She kept returning to the pen to check they were well, and up to the day they left for their new homes, she occasionally permitted the whole litter to gather around and have a quick milky drink!

"Cooper"
Photo: Becky Smith

Grooming & Vets

Spending Money ......

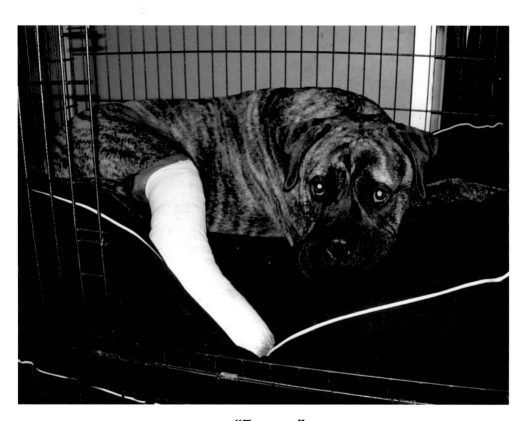

"Teagan"
Photo: Heather Waite

For some reason, the boldest dog becomes a quivering wreck when brought into a vet's waiting room. This has a certain logic, being scared of dentists myself I can see their point of view perfectly. Your sweet, biddable little dog suddenly turns into a flailing demon, claws gripping the floor and an absolute refusal to go anywhere near the place unless dragged in screaming. Administering medicine at home can also be awkward. Polly used to hoover everything vaguely edible in a few seconds, but crush a worm pill and she became immediately suspicious and would sniff it carefully before giving me one of her icy looks and stalking off to see what could be raided from the bin.

Less logical is their hatred of being shampooed. Is it the smell of being clean, the loss of dignity being rubbed all over with suds or the slippery surface of the bath? This will be the same dog that likes walking in the rain but the first sign of water from the shower attachment he screws his eyes up and panics as if acid has been dripped on his nose. That's if you can get him in the bath to start with – every dog becomes twice as heavy and ten times as awkward when it comes to getting him in there. Once in, most stay put, shivering pathetically as you get to work but as soon as it's over, they know that they can give a shake and soak you!

Shampoo and Setter

It's bath time, how I hate it
I know I'm full of grime
But water, soap and scrubbing
Just gives me a hard time!
Every month, it feels like
I must be soaked and smothered
With smelly stuff they call "shampoo"
I'm too old to be mothered!

So here I am, quite ready
To run away from this
By charging past the bathroom
I'll just give it a miss!
My owner's standing waiting
With a hand upon my collar
To make quite sure I can't escape
However hard I holler!

I'm trapped now, in the bathroom
I hear the taps are running
She has to get me in the thing
(Without damaging the plumbing)
She talks to me quite kindly,
But no doubt to her intent -
I know if I don't jump right in now
She'll be clear on what she meant!

Okay, I'll put my paws up
And look like I will jump
Then she'll grab my long back legs
And I'll fall in with a bump.
Once in, I stand quite still
There's just no point in fighting
I'll pull a sad face and whimper too
It's simply NOT inviting!

Now I'm soaked and dripping
I'm shaking, feeling cold
The water's stopped, the bottle's out
But I have to do as I'm told,
Standing still while she rubs it in
That bit's not too bad!
Then all rinsed off, and clean once more
Right down to each pink pad!

But now I'll wreak some revenge
On such a serious thing
For despite being wet and soggy
I feel happy enough to sing
Without a thought I'll leap out
And while she's still standing there
I'll shake just as hard as I can
She'll be soaked but that's only fair!

Once your dog is squeaky clean, dried off and brushed, trimming the nails finishes off the job nicely. That is, if you can get anywhere near the beast. Internet forums for dog owners are awash with pleas for help from owners who "can't cut the nails" on their dog and pay their complacent vet a small fortune to have it done, adding to the trauma for the dog and the owner's pocket. Living alone it is a real challenge as you battle to pin the dog down and clip nails without a sudden movement causing a mistake and blood pouring from the nail stump seemingly non-stop. Luckily, I am also a cat owner and whereas dogs pay no heed to their nails, cats spend most waking moments honing claws to needle points which they do not hesitate to use as weapons so once you've cracked it with a cat – a dog is relatively easy – in theory!

The following was inspired by "Duncan", owned by a long suffereing Ann MacDonald, a Dalmatian with more than his fair share of attitude ......

Nail Tale

I REFUSE TO HAVE MY NAILS CLIPPED
They're better being left alone;
I can grip the ground
So much easier, I've found
But my mum does nothing but moan!

She says they need to be trimmed
So we can look smart and well groomed
But I know when she's ready
With clippers held steady
My days as a slob-dog are doomed!

I REFUSE TO HAVE MY NAILS CUT
My mum's given up with the clippers
She tried once or twice
Telling me it was nice
But she lied, so I chewed up her slippers.

She then found a plug in device
With sandpaper – aghh! Hell beckons!
As it got up to speed
I bit through my lead
And was out of the door in two seconds!

I REFUSE TO HAVE MY NAILS DONE!
So my mum took me down to the vet
I defeated three nurses
And assorted curses
A sedative, some rope and a net!

My mum despairs of me now
My nails have become very long
I go clickety click
It's quite a good trick
And I don't see why that is so wrong!

Grooming parlours are just about everywhere now, so if all else fails you can send your dog for a few hours of pampering, although it is not always obvious that the dog sees it as such. Many groomers now offer a mobile service as well so they can come to your home instead.

"Dog wash? Us?"
Photo: Shelley Watson

I knew one groomer whose technique was to simply clip the entire coat off – the district filled up with unrecognisable Bichons, Old English sheepdogs and Lhasas which had been clipped of their coats for the summer as the owner "couldn't be bothered" to maintain the coat. I do wonder why such people choose a coated, high maintenance breed then try to turn it into something else. At the other end of the scale are the show exhibitors, to whom grooming has been elevated to an art form, and despite indications that they spend a lot of time on preparation at home, they can be seen working away for hours at the show benches until their exhibit is perfect. The dogs, clearly used to the routine, are always extremely well behaved as they are trimmed and brushed and sprayed and generally made into canine super models. No wonder the Standard Poodles, probably the most spectacular of highly groomed show dogs, look snootily at my "one-swipe-of-the-damp-cloth-and-he's-done" Dalmatian.

In a development of grooming, there has been a growth in "dog clothes" over recent years, inflamed by the glossy magazine images of celebrities with small dogs dressed in "human" clothes. Pet shops are quick to catch on and it now seems impossible to avoid it. Dogs can be dressed in County colours, army style kit, jumpers, hoodies and jeans, plus "designer" gear and bling. My dogs have waterproof quilted dog coats bought primarily for winter days for Polly when she got older and felt the cold more, also outdoor shows in wet weather when we have to stand around. These resemble horse rugs not human clothing and for scorching days I have silver reflective coats to keep them cool.

Fashion Victims

I really can't imagine why
It's become the thing, I cannot lie
To dress us up in human gear
Dresses, tops and worse, I fear
We all have the perfect coat
I'm not sure that all owners note
That should be enough for dogs
Without the need for fancy togs.

Trendy magazines, all ads
For the latest money making fads
Show "celebs" in careful poses
With dogs dressed up just showing noses
Designer gear, from what I see
But how do they manage to, well, pee?
Some think it makes the dog look cute
For me it's just one long big hoot

My beloved owner thinks it's rash
To part with large amounts of cash
To dress me up like a hairy dolly
I'm glad, it seems to be a folly
To alter what nature gave to me
It does the job just right you see!
My coat is clean and always shines
Much better than any designer lines.

And if I find a dog in clothing
I treat it with such scorn and loathing
I'll grin, and make it feel the pits
Although I can see the eyes are slits
With rays of malice between each blink
Shall I tell it what I really think?
But no, it's already doomed and hated
And my dear! What it's wearing is oh so dated!

But as I age it's becoming clear
I feel the cold with winter near
Some days when the rain is cold and lashing
And the wind is giving me a bashing
Then I'd be glad to be well covered
As long as I'm not completely smothered
Something waterproof, flashy and red
....Now I'll have to eat the words I've said!

On to veterinary matters. It seems that even "home treatments" such as giving a worm pill bring out the worst in the most placid dog. If you live alone, time to phone a friend! I think I have tried every method in the book and a few more besides; after many years I have still not cracked it. You can find the tastiest treat, the smelliest morsel, wrap it around a pill and the dog will instantly detect it and stalk off, My bitches would also glance back over their shoulder and give me "that look" which was one of disgust mixed with promises of total non-cooperation for at least an hour.

Even if you manage to get the pill down the throat, there is absolutely no guarantee that it will continue its downward journey and may often be found days later in a corner, having been discretely discarded.

The Bitter Pill

There's something been put in my food bowl
It's small and it's white and it's round;
It's hidden amongst the tinned dog meat
I don't think it's meant to be found.
She must think I'm stupid, my owner,
Assuming I'll eat it with glee
Which just goes to show that she's foolish
If she thinks she'll get *that* thing down me!

I wonder what cure this will give me,
A nice shiny coat, or wet nose?
I expect it will taste bad and bitter
It's certainly nothing I chose!
And disguising it badly in meat chunks,
Is simply unsubtle and mean,
Why not grind it right down to a powder
Then blend it in, so it's not seen?

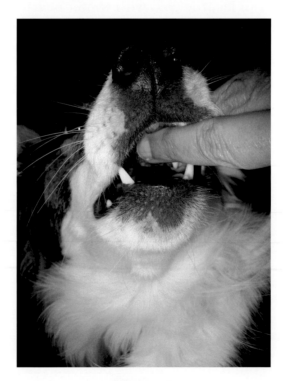

"Fudge"
Photo: Rachel Atkin

Mind you, my nose is so powerful,
It can seek out the smallest offence
Whatever she does to conceal it,
Is simply not making much sense
She might as well go for the force-feed
And ram in down hard in my throat
I'll show willing for barely a minute
Then sick it up on my clean coat.

She once tried a liquid variety
I just left the food in the bowl;
She bought a syringe from the pet shop
And squirted it in, oh how droll!
In less than a second her jumper
Was covered as I spat the stuff out,
With my mouth still wide open and grinning
I'd won that round, beyond any doubt!

But – maybe I'm ill and don't know it,
Or the pill is to stop something bad
I know that she wants what is best for me
So I ought to be grateful and glad
That she gives me something to help me
To enjoy life with maximum pleasure,
So I'll take a deep breath and eat quickly,
And spit it out later, at leisure!

From time to time things go wrong and an operation or procedure is called for. This may be the result of an accident or illness. My Dalmatian Polo had it both ways in 2006 just after Polly was buried. Grieving for his friend, so I assumed, he had a fit in front of me one evening and although it was soon over, it was a frightening thing to witness and he clearly didn't understand what was going on.

Despite medication, a month later he took another fit when he was loose on a walk and fell down a short cliff unconscious, landing in undergrowth at the side of a lake. By this time he had knocked down a dead tree, hurtled through a bramble bush and bounced off rocks and I was convinced he was dead. Eventually, two of us managed to slither down after him without ending up battered beside him and we slowly brought him to safety. Partly due to his portly figure at the time and the fact that he was relaxed, he escaped with missing and broken teeth, an assortment of rips and grazes, and some serious bruising.

More frightened than hurt, he was clingy and cautious for a while afterwards, but made a full recovery from his injuries.

Prior to these incidents, he developed trouble with his plumbing so had to spend two weeks in the veterinary hospital on a drip with tubes in embarrassing places, then he was neutered, then a problem was found with his eye; some dogs are just unlucky.

Whatever the problem, there is no doubt that every dog likes to be back home with his owner. Keeping a convalescing dog quiet though is quite another matter!

Coming Home

I'm coming back home tomorrow,
I've been away for a while,
To be taken quite ill
Was a shock, but still -
I'm *much* better now, by a mile!

Back home to the farm and freedom,
Instead of being banged up in town
In a cramped and cool cell
With no view! - oh well,
I did try hard not to get down.

There's been people here, coming and going
I'm now very used to their faces
There were needles and dressings
And tubing (no messing!)
Ending up in the strangest of places!

So my mum is due early tomorrow
With my welcoming friends in the car
It's goodbye to the vets
And the other sick pets
Then home thank you very much, ta!

I look forward to getting back home,
But although I am passed fully fit,
I think I'll pretend
I'm not *quite* on the mend
She'll be kept on her toes for a bit!

That should be worth lots of cuddles,
I know that she's truly missed ME!
Perhaps I'll sleep on her bed
Curled up by her head
For the rest of my life, you'll see!

"Teagan"
Photo: Heather Waite

Despite the rolling eyes, it is surprising how quickly dogs recover from routine ailments and operations. That is, from a veterinary point of view and all the time that you are out of sight. When you are solicitously changing bandages or giving medicine, it's quite a different story with moans and groans quite likely to have you scoop the dog into the car and charge off down to the vet again, where the patient will stage an immediate recovery at the sight of a needle!
I have always found that the males make the biggest fuss at the slightest ills; Polly was always a dreadful flirt with the vet regardless of pain or discomfort and once she discovered that he had a tin of liver treats for "difficult" and "brave" dogs, she took this to a new level!

"Skittle" takes a jump
Photo: John Young

Active Dogs

Showing and other dog hobbies

Let's hear it for the Cleveland Comets Flyball Team!
Photo of "The Proverbial Verbal" - Ziggy by John Clarke

For those who don't, competing with dogs is a complete mystery and for those who do, the results can be... a compete mystery! It is addictive, and like most addictions is a hard master at times. Getting up at 3am to drive to the other end of the Country, or to catch a ferry to another Country for the really hardened, requires a degree of dedication that my last boss longed for in my day job.

For the dogs, some like it, some don't. I had a bitch who was beautiful, trained up well but as soon as she saw a show ring, the tail went down and she crawled along on her belly. Once in the ring, she seemed to do the opposite of what was required to fully sabotage her chances. No amount of cajoling, threatening or coaxing could persuade her that it was a fun thing to do so she retired at the tender age of eight months and lived a happy life as a well-loved companion. So, Sky, the poem "Showing – Off!" is inspired by you. Another bitch was very promising as a puppy but decided that "flying" her ears back most unattractively was the way to get the judges attention and so it did – unfortunately he wrote her off as soon as he looked at her. Luckily, others took to it well and we had some great days out. However, harking back to mysterious results – "Polly" spent most of her career gaining second place despite the winner being different nearly every time but we had a lot of fun, and "The Alternative Winners" reflects that. Strangely, when she reached the age of eight I started to show her again in veteran classes and she suddenly developed a winning streak and enjoyed a brief, if late, career.

Showing is not the only game in town though, and hundreds of people make even bigger sacrifices in time and effort to compete in flyball, working trials, agility, heelwork to music, and obedience not to mention more specialist breed specific activities such as Husky racing (Siberian Huskies) and carriage dog trials (Dalmatians).

I make no apology for starting with showing, which is my main interest, this is a poem about a young bitch that really did not want to be shown and went to great lengths to sabotage any chances she may have had. A number of dogs simply do not want to be shown; they pick up the tension, don't like too many other dogs or simply feel overawed by it all. Unfortunately there are many cases where the owner ignores this and the dog becomes increasingly unhappy. A friend once commented to me that dogs don't ask to go to shows – we take them, so we can't expect them to always be happy about it. Sometimes, it is best to leave them at home and wait until one comes along who really loves it.

Showing?...Off!

I've been around for months on end
Seeing how much you will spend
Taking me to ringcraft classes
Having fun with lads and lassies
I guess you want me fit to show
Standing still, all square, ho ho!
Then trotting straight, but not too far
That's what YOU think! Ha ha ha!

I'll place my feet at "ten to two"
There won't be much that you can do
One leg forward, another back
Regardless of the "proper" stack
I'll stretch my back so I am LONG
So overall I'll look quite wrong
And curl my tail to form a "C"
I think that really flatters me!

I'll clamp my mouth shut good and tight
The judge will have a mighty fight
To see my teeth so white and clean
That's if I'm feeling not TOO mean!
Then there's the loose one, at an angle
Perhaps I'll simply let it dangle
All the time I'll twirl around
While you, my dear, daren't make a sound

I'll fold my ears back when I run
(And keep them there until I'm done)
I'm going to stop this silly lark
It seems that you've been in the dark
When you say "we're going showing"
I'll just reply "well I'm not going!"
I'd rather run and play and tease,
So can't we give this up now? Please?

Staying on the showing theme, some exhibitors can make a huge song and dance about their appearance, choosing clothes more expensive and flamboyant than they would buy for day to day life, matched with just the right shoes. Others turn up in jeans and casual top even at a top level show, which I have always considered to be an insult to the judge who is usually immaculately turned out as a tribute to the importance of the occasion. Once the outfit is chosen though, even more effort goes into "lucky" charms and accessories for many. Does it work? It's hard to tell!

I should be so lucky

Luck .... defined by the Collins Concise Dictionary as "events that are beyond control and seem subject to chance" . With dog shows this can range from turning up on time at the right venue (with the right dog) to finding that everyone else in your class has stayed at home. For some, luck is getting round the ring without attracting audible condemnation from the ringside, or wishing that the ground would open up under you as the puppy demonstrates your complete incompetence as a handler. Some people claim not to use or wear anything special in the ring, in the firm belief that luck is defined as going under a judge who likes your dog on the day and gives you a good placing.

That may be so, but some exhibitors do have special items of clothing or jewellery which they always wear in the ring to bring them luck, and such people range from the nervous novice to the regular CC winner. One person I know always wears a particular jacket which would, by now, not hold its own in the backroom of a charity shop but the owner still wears it, as she "feels naked without it". The mind boggles. Clothing may not always be obvious, either. Another exhibitor, and I use the term appropriately, wears knickers incorporating pictures of her breed. As a friend pointed out, was she expecting to "drop her kit in front of the judge ?" As far as I know, there have been no witnesses to this eye-catcher and her dog still pays her no attention in the ring. Next time you watch a class, remember that the most smartly dressed male exhibitor could be wearing their lucky Mickey Mouse underpants under those well-cut trousers!

Jewellery is popular with a number of people, particularly if given by someone special, and this can range from a smart pin to discreet earrings. Genuine horseshoes and gold medallions are more of a problem as clanking around the ring festooned with 5lb of ironmongery is more likely to bring *bad* luck as it catches the judges eye in the most literal sense. Black cat motifs are a common choice, but I'd rather have the real thing perched on the judges table, then my bitch might concentrate a bit, although so would the entire class as they looked in exactly the same direction regardless of where their bodies were pointing. Much safer are the tiny silver horseshoes, four leaf clovers and other charms which are of only limited embarrassment when they fall out of your pockets with the bait, unless your dog decides to swallow them which some are brainless/greedy enough to try!

Lucky shoes are also popular and are fine as long as you can actually run in them. One person bought a smart pair of ankle boots with a neat velcro fastening, "just for Crufts". During their trial outing at an Open show, the trot around a peat-floored indoor school was too much for the velcro which parted without warning and the boots were hastily abandoned on the second leg of the triangle. Sometimes though, apparently strange footwear is more to do with common sense than luck. I remember standing next to a very well-known exhibitor and judge at Birmingham, who was dressed beautifully as far as the ankles but sported the most hideous pair of trainers. "Well," she remarked, "at least I can run and my feet are comfortable." Shoes will also fall apart eventually, at which point the cry "heel!" takes on a new meaning as you flap round the ring trying to keep pace, and your cool, with the other four feet of the ensemble gleefully gathering speed in front of you. Am I superstitious ? Well, up to a point, but finding something suitable to wear or use is not that simple. I tried a rabbits foot round my neck for a while until the dog snatched it when doing his victory dance (in VHC position). I have tried lucky socks and a special jacket, which coincided with the longest run of cardless shows in our undistinguished career, then I changed to a different jacket, but kept the socks. Almost overnight we had our first win then a string of seconds....... then fourths ...... then back down to being chucked out.

I am reminded of the advertisement placed in a vet's waiting room about a lost dog - one ear ripped, castrated, lame, blind in one eye with a long scar down one side. Answers to the name "Lucky".

You have been warned.

Whatever the sport or activity, there is a solid core of entries from dogs and owners who never seem to progress very far. Why do they do it? I used to look forward to the mini competition inside the official one where I consider that I have had a good day if I beat a particular close rival. It may be part of someone's social life and they enjoy the chat and catching up with the gossip, as well as seeing other people's dogs and comparing notes on breeding, feeding and training. Or it may be just that they know that they will always have a good day out with their dogs.

The next poem is a tribute to those people who make up the bulk of entries at any competition, and support their breed or activity solidly

for years without making up champions or winning countless trophies.
Take a bow!

The Alternative Winners

Let's hear it, for the alternative winners
For those who never win classes
But enter each time
And will never whine
Or say that the judge needed glasses.

I'm often an alternative winner
My favourite colour is blue
Or yellow, or green
If you know what I mean
I obviously haven't a clue.

I was dragged round many a contest
Any time any place would do,
But at every show
Wherever we'd go
It was blue, blue, blue, blue, blue ...

I've been up to Crufts more than once,
I strutted my stuff in the ring,
My mum had a ball
And kept saying to all
We were *there*, and that was the thing.

Just to be placed was a thrill!
The winning did not really matter
And being thrown out
Though it counted for nowt
Didn't prevent a really good natter!

I've friends who do odd things like flyball,
Agility, obedience and dancing
They're not always winning
But they just keep on grinning
As they love all that jumping and prancing

So let's hear it, for the alternative winners
We all like to go, and look proud
While doing our best
As we're put to the test
We're all lovely, let's say it out loud!

Having Dalmatians has been my chief joy during my dog life so far, but even I was surprised to find that many of them are doing competition obedience, heelwork to music and agility. With the breed's reputation for being un-trainable and stupid, it can be an uphill battle against prejudiced trainers and nothing made me more proud than to find that Polo's son Skittle, a failed show dog and general idiot, had taken to agility in a big way and was finally achieving clear rounds. His owner Gail used to be a show jumper so walking courses, judging distances and going against the clock has been second nature to her. His house mate Nugget, another male Dalmatian, alternates between the show ring and Afghan racing – he even has his own racing jacket! Agility for him has remained a mystery.

The next poem is inspired by Skittle who loves his agility so much that he goes into a major song and dance routine each time the lead is brought out ready to be put in the car. I am very proud of his achievements, especially as he was virtually laughed out of the training hall when he first started. He now enjoys a keen fan club and I am looking forward to watching him compete. It is also an encouragement to others with ABC (Anything But Collie) breeds and types who would like to have a go, but are not sure that they can. There's only one way to find out - go for it!

Jumping For Joy!

It's that day again that I most treasure
To do things quite rare in my breed
I know 'cos she's opened the cupboard
And taken out my special lead!
It's the day that I do something special
And show all the rest I am no wally
For a big spotty clown can take part
In things normally done best by a Collie!

Yes, we're off to take part in Agility!
I'm just so excited and keen!
What will be first, the long tunnel?
Or taking some jumps, nice and clean?
I really don't mind what I'm faced with
It's such good fun, guessing what's next
And trying for that magic clear round
Then my mum tells her dog friends, by text!

When I started, the story was different
The other dogs laughed in my face
Because of my short coat and spotting
They always put me in my place
I couldn't work out what to do
I was scared, the jumps seemed so brittle,
The poles would go flying all over
No wonder my name is called "Skittle"!

My mum kept on going through training
Although I was not on the ball
And I'd tried oh so hard in the show ring
But had not really scored there at all
Then suddenly I found I could do it
I realised that this was the thing!
I began to get better and faster
And my heart began truly to sing!

We started to go in for contests
People would start pointing and staring
My kennel mate Nugget just laughed
He'd no idea how I was faring
I'd be flying the minute I started
And racing around the long track
With the audience suddenly silent
As I made them take their words back!

It's now my favourite pastime,
I'm even achieving clear rounds,
I dream of the jumps and the tunnel
Which I've mastered in leaps and in bounds
So whenever I'm having a bad day
And Nugget has stolen my toy
I just think I'll be off to agility
Where I know I'll be jumping for joy!

"The Proverbial Verbal" - Ziggy
Photo: John Clarke

It's a fair bet that whatever dog activity you take part in, there will be an "off" season over the winter months when plans for the coming season can be made for both dog and owner.

Dog clubs often note a rise in attendance after Christmas and for some owners, this is a golden opportunity to put the dog in the car, drive somewhere inhospitable and draughty, and hang around for ages waiting to be seen. Rather like going to an Open Show in winter, in fact. It also has the advantage of providing a welcome social occasion for both dogs and owners but at one club that we won't mention, this suddenly became something more as a dog briskly mounted a much larger bitch without either owner noticing. Even if your dog displays model behaviour during the entire evening, he will completely forget it as soon as you leave the hall.

Some members make a New Year's resolution that this year, they really WILL lose weight and get fit in time for the start of the main season in March. Contemplating the reading on the bathroom scales and the weather outside, one member vowed that he would start jogging, work on his handling and cure the dog of grinning inanely at the judge when he approached to look at the teeth – just as soon as the weather picked up a bit. And indeed it did – the following May.

Waiting to be judged at the PDSA Show
Photo: Emma Brackenridge

As dogs get older they slow down and eventually lose their sparkle but those with a long show career behind them still love to come out whenever possible, and there are "Veteran" classes to cater for them. To be a Veteran, a dog needs to be at least seven years old in the UK and eight years or over for Ireland. Polly's best result was 4th in the Veteran Stakes at the Saint Patrick's Day Show in 2006, the Irish Crufts, trotting up the green carpet under the spotlight with a commentary over the tannoy. It was a wonderful moment. Hannah, Polly's half sister, was not a big winner but absolutely loved being in the ring where her tail never stopped wagging.

Granny Hanny

My name's Hannah, I'm getting on now
A grandma too, what a shock!
But my eye still gleams
And my smile still beams
So nobody, ever, must mock!

I used to go out to shows
To trot round and all that stuff
But mum says it's time
As I'm past my prime
For lounging at home, that's enough!

I've enjoyed having puppies, it's true
I have a great life down on the farm,
But I hanker for showing
It's hard, not knowing
If I still could; where's the harm?

Excitement! We went out last week
A village show, just for some fun.
I held my head high
Under a lovely blue sky
And showed them all how it is done.

I've still got it, and boy was I proud!
And collected some lovely rosettes
Who cares that the winning
Was "waggiest tail" and "grinning"
Did I just love it? You bet!

A certain amount of training goes into a show dog, but for a real exhibition of training and skills take a look at obedience competitions. King of the ring must be the Border Collie, with the special high intelligence of the breed, and they are simply a joy to watch in action. There are many championships shows in Ireland where obedience and agility are on at the same time as the show classes so it is simply a matter of wandering to one end of the show ground to see these super stars of the dog world. I keep hoping that the performances will inspire mine to do better but so far, it hasn't worked.......

Working Day

My mother said I was a special pup
Born with a bigger brain and eagerness for work
Compared to others of my kind, although I don't see it
After all, what is intellectually challenging
In rounding up sheep? (stupid creatures that they are)
My mother rounds up sheep; Daddy on the other hand,
Does odd things that seem to require much thought
And precise, quick moves to no particular end.

I went to watch him work last weekend
Hours of waiting on a windswept field in the rain
Then herself led him out, attached by a rope
Which is never done when we are at home
But he didn't seem to mind too much this time
Holding himself alert and ready for anything
But not a sheep in sight, which was puzzling to me.
Perhaps they couldn't make it on this occasion.

All went quiet around the roped-off area
Our daddy was released from the length of rope
And sat motionless, with the wind softly lifting his coat
Ears pricked, waiting for a signal from herself.
Then off they went at a brisk walk straight down,
Then sharp left without warning, then right
Suddenly they stopped and herself walked away.
Daddy stayed put as if turned to stone; I would have fretted.

She called him; he came, and accurately sat beside her
I couldn't understand why he did this but people approved.
Some more manoeuvres with herself looking proud
As Daddy showed everyone how clever he is
He even picked out a cloth, from many set down
Bringing it back and handing it over willingly
Without any thought that it might be for him after all.
At the end, much noise as the watchers applauded.

Mother says that when I am older I will do this too
I can't wait to learn how to do these strange things
Even though it seems hard work, understanding herself
Sheep look so much easier to deal with I must admit
But herself tells us that I am special being Daddy's son

And I will bring glory by following in his footsteps
It would be good to carry on when he is too tired to continue
So I will practise and practise, until he's proud of me.

"River Run" owned by Jan Matthews
Photo: Jack Midgley

"It's a hard life being a dog"
Photo Dani Dinwoodie

Crimes and Punishments

Dogs doing what dogs like doing–driving you mad!

Zeus and Saski discuss who should have the chair
Photo: Michelle Thomis

Puppies think that everything is a game, so stealing things is fair enough! As a dog gets older, this habit can become hard to break and there have been some highly accomplished thieves. Although no malice is usually intended, punishment is sometimes given to the bewilderment of the dog who just thought it might be funny. The connection between crime and punishment is one that most dogs have never fathomed out so they just carry on regardless! Some simply never leave the puppy philosophy that everything is fair game ....

Grown Up

I'm a grown-up now, and sensible
Gone are the good old days
With pools on the floor
When I couldn't make the door
And other delightful ways.

I've given up chewing the furniture
A chair leg just isn't the same
Give me a rawhide
About six inches wide
Which is equally good, as a game.

I walk around now, quite content
To have all four feet on the floor
It's no longer right
To simply take flight
And run round the walls to the door.

Mealtimes are far more peaceful
Without having to bolt it at speed
I have time to savour
The delightful flavour
Which I missed before, through greed.

My owner says I'm much nicer
She now loves me even more
But it's boring being good
I've done all I should
Perhaps I should rip up the floor .....

When I worked on rescue the reasons why a dog "had to go" were many and varied, the saddest were where one person in the family was closely bonded with the dog, but the partner or other family member insisted that the dog was a nuisance, wicked, bad mannered and generally a pain so must go. This next poem was the first that I wrote – I am sure I'm not the first person to prefer a dog's company to that of another human!

Unwanted .....

I'm mad, I'm bad, I'm naughty all round
That's what my mum's new boyfriend has found.
He says he can't stand it, these games that I play
Whatever I do, I'm just in the way.
If I do something funny that might cheer him up
Like taking a drink of tea from his cup
Or hiding a shoe, his paper or tie
It results in his anguished, high pitched cry
"That dog must go! I can't take any more!
Get rid of him now – show him the door!"

I'm mad, I'm bad, I'm naughty all round
This man is now wanting me put in the pound
He can't stand the hairs, the mess in the place
Or the way that I'm always an inch from his face
My mum has been weeping, she loves me so much
And I love her too, with her kind gentle touch
But I can't get around this unfeeling man
Who wishes me gone, as soon as he can
And replaced with a refined, white standard poodle
(Not a breed that's been known to throw up dried egg noodle!)

I'm mad, I'm bad, I'm naughty all round
But I'll have to keep more than one ear to the ground
To hear what he's planning, a fate worse than death
To feel so unwanted I can barely draw breath
For all that I'm clowning around, I can see
This man is intent on just - dumping me!
I'm beginning to panic, it shows on my face
By tomorrow I could be away from this place
Leaving the person that I love the best
Because of her man, because I'm a "pest".....

I'm mad, I'm bad, I'm naughty all round
But my mum thinks I'm such a *wonderful* hound
We now spend each day just walking and roaming,
There's been no more talk of the pound or re-homing
I'm bouncy and lively, with such a big heart
And now we're together, we'll NEVER part
My days are just fun, I'm with my best friend
She'll be with me now 'til I get to the end
This is one friendship that'll last and last

... The boyfriend meanwhile is a thing of the past!

Elaine with Silk
Photo: Patch Guipago

Certain breeds have a tendency to steal food at every opportunity, despite being of model behaviour in every other respect. Step forward, Labradors and Dalmatians, you are top of the list of suspects when food is missing!

My Old Dog's a Dustbin

. .... and he wears a dustman's hat – or at least, he would if he hadn't eaten it. It's amazing what lengths some dogs will go to in order to steal food or in fact anything remotely attractive or different. Have you noticed that if you change your dog's food there is a whole range of ill-effects from straight rejection to violent bouts of sickness BUT if the substance is stolen it's a different thing entirely!

Thieving of food has always been a hazard to both dogs and owners although if the food is within reach, it must be simply SOOOOO tempting. One person reported that their dog had an "endless" list of crimes including three packs of butter, newly baked bread, shopping bags (still containing a supermarket shop). Another owner of many years experience claims to own the worlds naughtiest dog who insists on thieving anything and everything within reach - even raiding the vegetable plot when baby carrots and new potatoes appear. Food which apparently out of reach is not safe either – one particular bitch could open all the doors – both ways. The owners had a pantry with a "normal" door on it and one Christmas the turkey was cooked and allowed to rest in the pantry while the owner and several guests were having an aperitif. Nobody noticed that Sally was missing. When the cook returned to the kitchen to serve the "banquet" there was only the smallest titbit of the turkey left, from a seventeen and a half pound turkey. Sally was so incredibly bloated she couldn't walk into the garden to go to the toilet and for several days she had to be carried. The same accomplished thief was running through the park one day. A couple were sitting on the park bench and the lady had a bucket-type handbag. Sally ran past and without stopping managed to grab a bag of sweets out of the bag and run off – without breaking her stride. A similar incident occurred at a show; while walking past other exhibitors she just snatched a plateful of food without even jerking on the lead. At the time the owner was very new into the show-scene and was mortified, so just carried on and hid. So if you remember the incident and it was your food that was consumed let me know and I will arrange for the guilty party will buy you a sandwich to make amends.

There is another feature of food thieves - the unusual properties of the skin inside the mouth - akin to asbestos since items grilling merrily at several hundred degrees are whipped out and swallowed without the eyes watering or steam coming out of their ears! Barbeques ...... we won't even go there. Up and down the country, owners have barbeque kit gathering dust in the garage after the first attempt at slaving over hot coals for an hour to be left with half a burnt sausage while the dog rocks back on its haunches patting a bulging stomach and grinning.

Woody, Labrador Retriever, ever hungry!
Photo: Miss E. Heslop

Of course, some thieve and others just stand and watch.........

One bitch would not allow thieving by any of the others and it worked a treat. One day, the owner's husband (who is usually tidy) left a strip of bacon drooped over the edge of the work surface. He then went out for a few hours leaving all the dogs in the same room. On our return this bitch was found standing with her nose pointing to the bacon and all the rest sitting neatly in their beds drooling. Needless to say they got the bacon as a reward.

Dogs have a strange definition of food sometimes. Various items have been eaten over the years, for example Oscar stole the remote control for the television that did weird things whenever he walked past it for a few days. Another demolished the Sky controller which had sat in the same place unmolested for two years, causing untold anguish with her owner who discovered that they are expensive to replace and take 28 days to arrive. Portia always thieved knives & forks, Polly actually swallowed a teaspoon which had some shepherd's pie attached to it. Many items of footwear are reported including an expensive pair of slippers, ok they were left out but why not the ageing trainers fourteen inches away? Duncan stole and ate a woollen sock which had to be removed surgically, Mouse stole the biggest Koi Carp he could find and dutifully buried it down the back of the settee. Poppy opened the sitting room door, found a laptop computer, and with an accomplice demolished the power supply. Luckily it wasn't connected to the mains at the time.

So how do we prevent this crime wave apart from locking the dogs up all the time? (My dog can whip a shoe into his bed virtually under my nose without my knowledge). The main problem is intelligence coupled with sheer greed; there are countless stories of breadbins being opened and the contents scoffed, one bitch was able to reach the tray that the toaster stood on, pull it closer to the edge of the work surface so she could grab the hot toast just as it popped up.

One solution offered was to precariously balance baking trays on a work surface, containing some choice food. One owner decided to try it; the result was an enormous clatter, dented baking trays and an unperturbed dog eating the 'bait'! Over time this will "train" a dog to take things VERY CAREFULLY so as not to knock things off the work top! Another owner not only ended up with dented and scratched baking trays but they were found beneath the trees at the bottom of the garden, together with saucepans which had been removed from the cooker. One was caught in the act of eating a roulade with his neck carefully craned over the top so as not to send the plate crashing to the floor! At least it saves broken china. Another deterrent offered to the owner of a particular serial offender was to make up a vile mixture of curry paste & Tabasco sauce to give him a "treat" that he found horrible but as he had already wolfed his owner's hot curry this had limited success!

Being a dustbin has its downsides, not least the vet's bills although my own vet gives a discount for entertainment value. What goes in, must come out they say which reminds me of a friend who lost a pair of marigold gloves. Picking up the dollops from the lawn one morning, she was horrified to find small yellow pieces in one pile, and checked her

A Chinese Shar Pei orders .... A Chinese!
Photo: Jules Furbank

dogs for signs of illness. It was only when she poked the mess to have a better look that she discovered where her marigolds had gone ..... but which of the wagging trio was guilty she never knew!

My mother had a simple answer to the problem of theft by the dogs – don't leave it out! It was the best incentive to clear up that we ever had. However, I have a friend with several Dalmatians who thought she had seen everything, until they acquired a particularly large and intelligent male. Wondering how he managed to steal when all the doors were shut, she was astounded one day to catch him opening doors. Not too difficult for the average dog, you may think, except that the door handles were not the lever type, but round knobs!

I currently have a very strange dog who, when offered a treat, takes it politely then spits it out in disgust. I found him in the kitchen one day sitting in front of the fridge, with the door open - nothing was touched. Now that doesn't seem normal ....

Biscuit in My Cheek

Strolling round the kitchen
I thought I'd have a look
In case some twit
Had left a tidbit
'Cos really I'm a crook!

I spotted fresh baked cakes
Cooling on the side
And grabbed one quick
With one deft flick
Then hid it with great pride.

Oh no! She's here, I'm caught!
My mum began to yell
"You wicked dog
You're just a hog
You've had your tea as well!"

She wrenched my mouth wide open
I stood and shook in shame
She grabbed the cake
I thought I'd take
And told me, I'm to blame!

I showed her I was sorry
My tail and ears sagged low
My eyes were sad
I'd been so bad
I just could not say no.

I slunk out to the garden
Then a glint came to my eyes
The biscuit, though bruised
Was lodged under my flews
.....I still had second prize!

Puppies are often moved on because of chewing up everything in sight. Ignorant owners don't realise the agony of teething and the puppy's need for relief and nothing is sacred to their hot stinging jaws. As they get older, some are shut away for hours on end so chewing becomes a sign of boredom. Whatever the reason, dogs find it hard to understand why destroying an entire kitchen brings terrifying reactions and revenge from owners.

"Norman"
Photo Shelley Watson

Choose Chews

I like to gnaw and bite all day
With new teeth coming through
I don't care what it is I chomp
A belt, a toy or shoe,
Or even kitchen cabinets
If it's all the same to you!
This obsessive demolition trait
Is simply what I do!

My gums are raw and bleeding now
I just can't help being blue
Some pointy teeth have just appeared
I've big ones coming too
I need to bite to ease the pain
While teeth are still so new
It's natural, or it's wickedness
Depending on your view

So don't tempt fate when I'm about
I haven't got a clue
I can't determine, or work out
What's valuable to you
So lock me up in my own space
And don't get in a stew
Throw me chunks of dried rawhide
So I can just choose chews!

Boarding kennels – there are good and bad, and for anyone contemplating using them, have a good look round first. I have been fortunate in finding the good ones when I have needed to, however there are some that are not as good and the dog thinks he is being punished. One dog went into kennels while the owner was temporarily homeless and when he pined and refused to eat, the kennel staff did nothing to coax him to eat. Eventually he was reunited with his owner and was soon back to normal.

Doing Time

What have I done to deserve this?
I can't remember a thing
Was it chewing the shoe
Drinking from the loo,
Or burying my mum's diamond ring?

All I know is that I've been sent down
For some unknown, unwitting crime,
I was put in the car
We didn't drive far
To the place I was put to do time.

They call this bleak place "boarding kennels"
It's simply a number of cells
I heard, with a pang
The gate shut with a clang
I was left, with all deaf to my yells

The food I was given was normal
But I didn't trust anyone there
So I turned up my nose
And starved; I suppose
It was saying I just didn't care

Then one day my owner came back
I could see the car parked up the hill
I jumped in and sat tight
Hoping she might
Not put me back through the mill!

I still don't know what I've done wrong
It was hell being banged up I admit
So for a month (or a week)
I'll be happy but meek
After that? I'll just live on my wits......

If you are away a lot at weekends in the summer, the garden is likely to be neglected and the weeds reach new heights and the neighbour's comments plumbed new depths. By winter it is a sad mud patch with sundry debris and yellowing stalks, with a scattering of chewed toys and old trophies from raids on the laundry basket. (so that's where my red sock/oven mitt/jogging bra went to!) The dogs think it's great and come back in with shining eyes and bi-coloured coats. Or tri-colour, if you're really unlucky. One owner had her garden landscaped into a neat lawned area where the dogs could only go if supervised, and a hard surface area where they could play freely and unattended. During a particularly hard winter they were banned from the fenced off lawn, and the owner was mystified when she found that the pads on her puppy were literally frozen when they came back in. A casual glance from the warmth of the kitchen revealed her youngest skating stylishly across the top of the fish pond and she fully expected her neighbours to pop up at the fence awarding marks out of ten! They now go to the park more often where for some reason the grass never seems to get cut up and the water rarely freezes over.

Fun in the garden
Photo: Eleanor MacDonald

Gardens are a great source of fun and opportunities for mass destruction to puppies. Forget your flowers, they will be eaten or trampled underfoot, shrubs make ideal places to hide and leap on, both resulting in odd shapes – usually flat. Ornaments will be toppled and smashed, canes chewed and sheds suffer un-repairable damage from scrabbling paws. As for the lawn, just don't expect to have it for long and possibly never again. Holes will be dug, apparently random but obviously highly significant spots (to the puppy) will be used as a toilet at every opportunity. If you have older dogs, they will probably assume that this is acceptable behaviour and join in with great enthusiasm. Polly specialised in snapping flower heads off and had developed it into an obsession, even to the point of removing the heads off the daffodils one day outside a neighbour's house while we were waiting for the doorbell to be answered.

I had an enquiry for a puppy from a woman who informed me knowledgeably that she was getting the puppy in the summer months when it wouldn't be dragging mud into the house on it's feet. Doesn't it rain in the summer occasionally? She hadn't even considered the inevitable damage to the garden itself. Needless to say, I didn't sell her a puppy!

Fudge remembering old friends.
Photo: Rachel Atkin

Finally.........

Time to say goodbye

Photo: Becky Smith

It happens eventually but we all dread it.

Whether it is by accident, illness or old age there is nothing that can prepare us for losing a dog. Having been through it once, I am told that it will be no easier when I lose the next one but I will never give up keeping dogs to avoid this experience, as I would be missing out on so much while I have them.
At the time of writing, friends also lost dogs in various circumstances and no one was more heartbreaking than another. I have tried to cover most circumstances here, death by old age, illness, and accident - the latter being particularly unkind - and I am sure that those of you who have lost a dog this way still miss them terribly.

I have also not forgotten the other version of bereavement – the solitary owner dying and leaving the dogs to an uncertain future. It is frightening just how many people have not considered this possibility so whatever age you are, please ensure that plans are in place for your dogs after you have gone – you don't know what tomorrow will bring – and you would want them to be happy and settled, wouldn't you?

The first poem was my first venture into this subject, and is a reflection of my experience with the loss of the family's Labrador retriever, Judy, who was a rescue dog. She was a great all round dog and as she became older and developed more problems, my mother agonised over whether it was better to let her go or allow nature to take it's course. Still undecided, she came down one morning and Judy would not get out of bed. My mother telephoned work and said she wouldn't be in, as she knew the time had come. She held Judy's paw for a while, then Judy gave a half bark, then silence. My mother did not know whether she was asleep, or had gone. Her body was warm, her eyes closed, and eventually she slipped away peacefully. There was no dog after Judy, all her toys and bed were disposed of so there was no further trace of her. My mother died in June 2002 and I would like to think that she and Judy are together again.

I hope that this section gives some comfort to those who have lost their dogs however long ago it was, and a tiny bit of reasurrance to those yet to go through the whole tragedy, that you are not alone and grieving for a dog is not a weakness. Your dogs gave you endless joy and will never be forgotten.

Sunset

It's sunset, and I'm ready to go
The light is now fading fast
It's time to say
Goodbye to the day
And to think once more of the past.

Don't you look upon me so sadly
I've had a really good life
I'm so sorry to leave
But please don't grieve
I'm going to a place free from strife.

Remember the day that we met
Coming home I was sick in the car
Then was chased by the cat
I didn't like that!
But I was soon your favourite, by far.

You've always been with me, my friend
Up hill and down dale on long walks,
In good times and bad
We've been happy and sad
I listened when you wanted to talk.

But twelve years have passed by in a flash
And the sun has gone, leaving a glow
Please hold me tight
As I go into the night
To the bridge, where my friends are, I know.

Remember that I'll always love you
I know that you'll never forget me
But one day you'll find
Another of my kind
And I'll be with you again, you'll see .....

"Judy" Chester, Labrador Retriever, 1976 – 1988

Sometimes, with the best care in the world, accidents happen with tragic consequences. I have known of several people that this has happened to and it must be the worst thing in the world to happen. If you have children, or visitors, extra vigilance is needed as gates and doors can be left open, bolts left off or not properly fastened, and in a few seconds the dog has gone out to the most dangerous place possible – the road. This poem doesn't relate to any one particular incident, but simply describes one possible version. However blameless the owner is, like many similar situations, the feelings of guilt seem to last for ever.

Taken

I can't believe that she's gone
I turned my back just for one second
I was sure she was still standing here
But an open gate clearly beckoned
She slipped away, (I didn't see her)
For adventure, on the open road
The place where she wasn't allowed
She didn't know the Highway code!

My boy came rushing in, gasping
"She's not here! Gone! Where is she?"
The lane so quiet through the day
Was suddenly too busy, to see
A small dog running loose and scared
Thinking now it's a stupid idea
To go and explore the wide world
With cars and trucks passing, so near.

I froze, then dashed out to the road
Through the open and still swinging gate
A bus was stopped, right on the bend
I knew then it was far too late
I saw her lying down on the ground
As I reached the sad, tragic scene
There wasn't a mark on her coat
No sign where the death blows had been.

I fell to the ground in anguish
Perhaps she was simply knocked out?
But the eyes that once shone so brightly
Were dull and there was no doubt

It was too late and some of the crowd
Knowing she was so gentle hearted
Muttered words of sympathy, knowing
She was gone, taken from us, departed

Some kindly folk helped me get up
They carried her back to the lawn
Tea was made, but was never drunk
My boy sat alone, too forlorn
I could not give him comfort, at all
Or utter a single kind word
It was too soon, and breathlessly sad
By then the whole village had heard.

We buried her under a tree
The whole event passed in a whirl
Quite soon we'll carve her a plaque
We'll never forget our poor girl
Every day, I can't help but think
She was taken, for the sake of a bolt
And a small voice adds guilt to the grief
It was your fault, your fault, your fault.....

Photo: Author

It came as a surprise to me just how few people have made provision for their dogs should anything happen to them. You don't know what tomorrow will bring. It's bad enough to lose a dog, but what will happen to them if you are suddenly not around? I hope that the plans I have put in place will not be needed for a long time but at least they are in place.

I wrote the following to draw attention to this possibility, it is also a tribute to the many voluntary organisations that do so much good work in this area.

Changes

It's nearly time for tea, I think
But she who feeds is still asleep
She nodded off some time ago
We missed our walk, she must be tired
No amount of nudging her
Speaking most persuasively
Could rouse her from so deep a slumber
We've tried our best but still she sleeps
We'll have to try another trick
This really isn't good enough!

My young friend here has given up
Mournfully, he's lying down
Waiting for her to stir, and rise
Then we'll know that all is well.
I am sulking, hungry now
How can she sleep so long and sound?
Then a dreadful fear comes over me
I creep back up and sniff her hard
There's something wrong, she's gone from us
She's cold, no breath moves in her breast.

I tell my friend, our tails droop low
He lets out a howl, so long and sad
Who will feed us, take us out,
Now we've lost our greatest friend?
We lie down, in a state of shock
The night is long, and full of horror
Morning breaks, but the scene remains
Like some morbid play or film
But what are we to do today?
Instinct says we stay right here.

The day drags on, we can't get out
Our water bowls are long since drained
We're sitting on either side of her
Protecting her from …. not sure what
Maybe if we hope and wish
This will have been a dream, no more
And her eyes will open, then she'll say
"Come on boys, let's go out!"
But another day draws to a close
And still she sleeps, this is no dream

We doze awhile, then comes a knock,
A hammering upon the door,
We bark until we're hoarse, and growl
Trying to tell those at the door
About the disaster, here within
A face appears, white with shock
Silence; then a mighty crash
As the door gives way and men rush in
Our mistress takes no notice now
For it has been too late for help.

She is carefully carried out
We want to stay close by her side
But hands appear and grab our collars
"Come with us", a small voice says,
"We will take good care of you,
We have some friends for you to meet
We'll soothe you and we'll find another
Good enough to treat you right"
We whine, we fear some cold dark days
As the life we know is snatched away.

Three months on and life is good
We're together in a brand new home
Although the pain won't fully die
Life carries on with new routines
And sometimes when the wind is blowing
I hear her voice, so quiet and soft
Telling me we're not to worry
I lift my head and sniff the air
I know she's glad that we are safe
We know she's watching over us.

The decision to say goodbye is the hardest one to make. My late mother knew that her Labrador Judy was coming to the end of her days, but no amount of reassurance that it was "kinder" to let the vet do the necessary deed made the decision easier. Although Judy was losing her dignity and quality of life, my mother could not bring herself to call the vet and beat nature to it.

She said afterwards that she still didn't know whether she did the right thing by letting Judy hang on until she couldn't sustain life any more. Would it have been kinder to have her put down? However, for a dog to die peacefully in her own bed with her owner can't be a bad thing ......

Losing Polly, my first dog, was a dreadful experience and my friends tell me that it doesn't get any easier after the first. Polly enjoyed life to the very end, went with dignity and no fuss, which is probably how she would have planned it if anything so fanciful could happen. I wrote "Immortal" a few weeks later having heard about a friend in the UK losing a bitch of a similar age and equally suddenly. We both wept.

With Polly I knew she was on a countdown and I had bullied the vet into telling me what symptoms would indicate that she had reached the end. When the symptoms appeared most dramatically and unambiguously, I knew when I rang the vet what the verdict would be so I was prepared, in a way. In other ways we are never prepared and at the time of writing, Polo is succumbing to his brain tumour and very soon I will need to make the call on that, before his quality of life diminishes irrevocably. I am dreading it.

Before publication, the moment came and I have now lost my special beautiful boy who is now buried next to Polly. People were incredibly kind about it, apart from two who were vile – but as someone remarked, "they loved him too" .... the owner is not the only one who is deeply saddened.

"Immortal" came to me in a rush, it was as though it was being dictated to me as I typed frantically, and was done all in one go. Perhaps Polly wrote it herself – I wouldn't be at all surprised! She also stirred me into putting this book together as it suddenly had an aim – celebration of the life of our dogs. Sleep well, Polly.

Immortal

I always knew that I'd live for ever
I never left the puppy stage;
Apart from honing certain skills
Like stealing, going "deaf" and more
I've always bounced when I should walk,
I've never trotted back when called
A meal is just five seconds long
It's been like this, nine years or more.

The past few months have been a drag
Keeping up with fitter dogs
I'd need a rest at some quiet spot
Before I'd leap up, tail wagging
And trot again like nothing happened
Apart from staying close to you
Just to stay the course, you see
And prove that all is well and good.

I've some discomfort on and off
I feel a little stiff on rising
But I know I'm going to live forever
So I ignore these warning signs
That whisper to me now and then
I'll show you that I'm just the same
But you keep looking at me oddly
Don't worry about me, I'm just fine.

Oh dear - I've been so sick tonight
It must have been some food I stole
I didn't get outside this time
Before I was very ill again
I expect we'll go and see the vet
He's lovely and kind, so I'll wag my tail
Even though really I feel quite bad
I trust him so I'll soon be better.

My owner is talking softly to me,
So is the vet, and the nurse is in tears
I stare at them, not afraid in the least
For I know I'll be fine, and have no fear
And now I have moved to a glorious place
I can keep a close eye on those I have left
I'll never be gone, I've just changed address
I'm immortal, I'll always be watching........

Polly (1996 - 2006) and friends

Photo of Polly by Amy Cauldwell

Roll of Honour

To our best friends who are no longer with us, thanks to everyone who has contributed to this memorial.....

Melissa, Cavalier King Charles Spaniel, age 5
Melissa you will always be in our hearts run free. Jasmine Houghton

Tala, Chocolate and Cream Miniature Poodle aged 3.
You were my forever dog, miss you always, wait for me. Mum xx

Jess, Lab X, age roughly 13
The best camping and hiking companion I could ever have asked for, sadly missed.

Bo, Shar Pei, age 4
Forever in our hearts, sadly missed by all, love you. Mum and Dad xoxox

Bonnie, English Springer Spaniel, 15 years old
Forever missed, never forgotten x

Ludmilla, Borzoi, age 12
Our darling Golden Oldie. You are always on our minds and Mum and Dad miss you so much xxxx

Amber, Golden Cocker Spaniel ran free 26.11.03
The 'happy' boy who left us far too soon. Until we meet again xxx

Daisy-May, Poodle x Lab, age 19 1/2 years old
Bridge 28/02/99 at 5.15pm
You were, are, and always will be my heart and soul
Patch G

Tawney, Utonagan, age 11.
My girl with a difference. Still sadly missed.
Crossed over to Rainbow Bridge Jan 23 2006 at 11.45am
Wait for me

Bumble, Mishu and Ted, my gorgeous Shibas, all aged 9 years
all lost to cancer. Lots of dogs have died, I know, but you were mine, and I miss you so xox

Steffi, JRT, age 12
Night night baby, we miss you so much
Jeff & Gail. XX

Jackson, Labrador Retriever, 8 yrs
Rest in peace little man, we'll meet again xxx

Spring, Australian Kelpie, 8yrs
You were a shining star that's why the heavens are bright xxx

Max, Australian shepherd x, Nov 1997 to May 2002.
Our time together was not enough. A brave boy to the end.

Cleo , (Ch Hyclough Cleo At Jomihvar)**,** Dalmatian died aged 14 and three quarters. A very special girl, and a joy to live with. Also **Carrie**, (Jomihvar Carrie Be Ann), Dalmatian, died at 9 and a half years. So sensitive to others and not fully appreciated 'til she'd gone. Joan & Mike Richardson

Tom, Border Collie, passed away 09/02/06 age 12
Miss you everyday, definitely one in a million!

Barney, X-Breed, aged 15, crossed the bridge 21/4/06
Never a day goes by when I don't think of my best friend. See you again one day my special lad.

Goldie Collie x Retriever aged 10
My beautiful lazy best friend, I miss you terribly
Ran to Rainbow Bridge in June 2001 Alex XXX

Winston Dobe x Rottie aged almost 12 years
Left me Sept 2005, your were the best friend I ever had....
still missed every day love Muma xx

Olly, (Cotwells Olly Oh No) Dalmatian, died aged 16.
A great gentleman. Also **Megan** (Cotwells Homelea Megan) Dalmatian, died 11 years. A lovely girl. Browning's Dalmatians.

Toffee, Beagle, age 2
Taken away too soon, still miss you after all these years
I'll see you again Gill xxx

Sam, Border Collie cross age 20
"Only" a farm dog but what a great character
Owen and Marie

Ginnie, cocker spaniel age 5
Sadly lost after whelping
You took your babies with you
My heart is still broken Gina xx